CRUSH IT!
CONQUER WORKPLACE CHALLENGES

A Practical Guide
to Overcoming Workplace
Challenges and Achieving
Professional Excellence

WRITTEN BY
RENE MADDEN

For more information, email rene@uplfitcareercoaching.com.

ISBN: 979-8-218-27643-0

Dear Reader –

I wrote *Crush It! Conquer Workplace Challenges* to help you overcome the difficulties I have faced in the workplace during my over 35-year career in the asset management industry but these action steps can be successfully utilized in every industry.

Over the years, I have experienced being overlooked for promotion, being pushed out of a position, working with bully bosses, and getting some challenging feedback from managers. I have learned how to conquer this opposition and I am passionate about helping others crush similar barriers they are facing.

This book is a hands-on guide which includes creating a career assessment, landing the job of your dreams, dealing with bad bosses, getting promoted, dealing with stress in the workplace, managing diversity, equity, and inclusion, taking your vacation, and not letting anyone steal your power.

In each chapter, I give real examples of what I dealt with and how it was handled. At the end of each chapter, I give action steps you can take if you are dealing with the same or similar challenge.

You can use this book repeatedly as you advance through your career and deal with challenges. A companion workbook is also available that can be used alongside the book so that you can take notes, put together goals and take action.

I look forward to hearing about your success as you put these principles into action.

Please contact me with feedback or questions
at Rene@upliftcareercoaching.com.

DEDICATION

To my dearest Jenna, Tara, and Ryan,

As I wrote these pages, my heart is filled with immense love and pride for each of you. This book, a testament to the resilience and strength we have all cultivated in our own unique journeys, is not just a reflection of my experiences but a dedication to the three extraordinary individuals who have made my life immeasurably meaningful.

Jenna, my firstborn, your unwavering determination, and passion have always been a source of inspiration. You face challenges head-on, fearlessly charting new territories in pursuit of your dreams. Your perseverance has shown me that success lies not just in reaching the destination but also in the unwavering spirit that propels us forward.

Tara, my angel and creative soul, your ability to see opportunities amidst obstacles is awe-inspiring. You navigate through ambiguity with grace, embracing change as a steppingstone toward growth. Your resilience has taught me the importance of adapting and staying open to the endless possibilities that life has to offer.

Ryan, my youngest, your quiet strength and dedication are a beacon of hope in turbulent times. I know you will lead with compassion, empowering those around you with your unwavering support.

Through my own challenges in the workplace, I have learned that it is not the absence of difficulties that defines us, but rather, the way we rise above them. In the pursuit of building meaningful careers, the path may be riddled with obstacles, but the strength of character each of *you has displayed in your own lives gives me the courage to share these experiences openly.*

As you embark on your own journeys, I hope this book serves as a guiding light, offering solace during times of struggle and reminding you that every hurdle is an opportunity to grow stronger. May it remind you that you have the power to overcome any challenge that comes your way, and that success is defined by the resilience with which you face adversity.

Remember, my children, life's greatest triumphs arise not just from victories but from the lessons we learn along the way. I dedicate this book to each of you, with the profound hope that it may serve as a beacon of hope and strength, lighting your path towards a future filled with courage, determination, and an unwavering belief in your boundless potential.

With all my love,

Mom

Get Your Free Crush It! Workbook

To get the best experience with this book, you can download my free Crush It! Workbook. This is a companion to the book to guide you through the action plans you can take to achieve the success you desire.

Download your free copy now by visiting:
https://upliftcareercoaching.com/crushit

TABLE OF CONTENTS

FOREWORD

"Crush It!" in the complex world of financial corporations requires fortitude, resiliency, artful communication skills, a change mindset and strong leaders and mentors to guide you on your journey. With 30+ years of practical, real-life experience in both management and individual contributor roles at four financial firms, Rene provides heartfelt and practical words of wisdom for people just starting their careers or facing challenges in their current career.

At these culturally distinct firms, each of Rene's roles gave her opportunities and challenges. Her direct and plain-English style enables the reader to clearly feel her passion and hear her lessons. She also covers a breadth of topics from understanding yourself and your goals to how to apply your skills using real-world, authentic behaviors. Finally, Rene's depiction of some of the nuances within the corporate environment, examples of how situations play out and how you might approach them and the shifting culture to embedded inclusion practices, can give you a taste of how her journey unfolded and give you some tips on how to address yours.

My career and expertise in financial services is managing and gaining agreement on change that is driven wholly by shifting market and client needs. Each firm, and professional within the firm, must be poised to set itself apart from the competition consistently. After working with Rene for five years, I know she is grounded in that mindset....and, most importantly, understands how to navigate success within that complex environment where you are expected to make a positive impact each and every day.

By Stacey Panagakis – Stacey's experience ranges from starting up a media company and talent incubator focused on driving artist and brand collaborations to leading marketing, operations and strategy roles at a Fortune 50 financial services firms for 20+ years

INTRODUCTION

I have had a very long and relatively successful career in the investment management industry. I fell into the industry by mistake many years ago back in 1987 – yes, the year the market crashed, on October 19, 1987. I was working for *Butcher and Singer*, a brokerage firm, at the time.

When I say I fell into the industry by mistake, I mean that I had no idea what I wanted to do after I quit my job at a real estate firm. It was right after my father's 60th birthday. He said to me, "I need to get my plot for the cemetery". I said, "Dad, 60 is too young to be thinking about dying!" Little did I know my dad would die nine years later, but that's another story. The one thing it did make me think about at the time was that I needed to figure out what I wanted to do with my life.

I was 23 years old, and I had just quit a job after only two weeks. It was the third job I had that year, but not my last. I actually ended the year having worked in five different jobs. My brother joked that I would have fun with my tax returns with all the W2s I would need.

You must understand, I was not a star student in high school, and I did not have a whole lot of ambition for college. I was the daughter of Italian parents and they thought that a girl did not really need to go to college. They thought I could just get a job as a secretary and be happy until I found a man who would marry me.

After high school, in the summer of 1982, I started working as a secretary at *The Philadelphia Saving Fund Society* (PSFS), a well-known bank in Philadelphia at the time. I started in the secretarial pool during my senior year of high school and got a job after I graduated, working for the assistant treasurer of the bank. If you are old enough to remember the movie *Nine to Five*, my boss was very similar to Dabney Coleman's character. He would hold out his mug for me to get him coffee. I used to roll my eyes at him and tell him, "That is not my job!"

I had a lot of fun working at the bank during my first year there. They used to call me the "social butterfly" because I was always talking to everyone in the office and having a good time (while always working hard when needed, of course!). However, at some point in my second year there, I became bored with my job. I knew I needed to do something different. After talking with some of my colleagues, I enrolled at Saint Joseph's University, majoring in accounting.

I began to have some purpose and goals in my life. I went to college at night for the next eight years. I also moved around to many jobs until I landed at a small asset management firm in Philadelphia. It was called *1838 Investment Advisers*. It spun off from *Drexel Burnham* right as Michael Milken went to jail.

I learned a lot during my time at *1838*. My title was Portfolio Accountant, but my role was a hybrid of functions including reconciling accounts, client service, systems liaison and I even handled their phone system. I wore many hats which helped me learn about what I liked to do and what I didn't like to do. I spoke to portfolio managers to learn the business, mostly focusing on fixed income, and gained insight into the workings of the portfolios as I started reconciling clients' portfolios. At the same time, I familiarized myself with different technologies. I learned how to write reports and how to navigate the portfolio accounting system that we used. Ultimately, I discovered that I really liked the investment management industry.

In 1993, after five years with *1838*, I got married, and moved to New York City, and started working at Morgan Stanley (*MS*). I had never even heard of this company, but it was all my new husband spoke about – how awesome it would be to work for one of the largest and most prestigious investment companies in the world.

Working at a large firm like MS was definitely a real challenge for me after having been part of a small firm. I was a big cheese at *1838* and I wore many hats. When I went to *MS*, I was just a small fish in a sea of many other fish.

I faced many challenges during my almost 20 years at *MS*, but I do feel I learned a lot from these challenges. In particular, I discovered what I truly wanted to do – help others be successful. Therefore, I am writing this book. I want to give others a guide on how to overcome challenges in the workplace, so they can be happy, have less stress in their lives and be successful….as defined by them.

CHAPTER 1

IDENTIFYING WHAT YOU WANT TO DO IN YOUR CAREER

"Your work is going to fill a large part of your life, and the only way to be truly satisfied is to do what you believe is great work. And the only way to do great work is to love what you do"

Steve Jobs

I never knew what I wanted to do or be in my career. I never had the passion for one thing. When I was child, I remember I wanted to be a nurse because I liked the idea of caring for sick people. However, as soon as I found out that I would need to see blood, my plan went right out of the window.

I was an okay student, getting mostly B's, and envied the smart kids. I just did not have the attention span. I think I may have had ADHD, but that was not a thing when I was young. I ended up not going to college right away, which was okay, because I took my time, going to school at night and working during the day.

I figured out the things I liked and those things I did not like along the way. I started managing people when I was at *MS*. It was not something I had aspired to, but it turned out I was actually good at it. One of the first teams I managed at *MS* was a client service team. This team was characterized by staff turnover and manual processes. I ultimately turned things around to build it into a valuable client service team. It was a magical mix of exciting work and fabulous people.

Because I didn't have a systematic way to assess my career goals, I just fell into roles. I figured out what I wanted to do as I was moving from job to job. Now I definitively know that developing a plan is a much better way to drive your career. If you are just starting out in your career, developing a list to assess what you are good at and what kind of things you like to do is essential...And it will continue to be important as you travel through your career. Here are some questions you can ask yourself:

1. **Do you like numbers?** Are you good at math? Do you like following the market? If so, maybe finance or accounting may be areas that you would be interested in.

2. **Are you a good writer?** Are you creative? Marketing may be a good career for you as you need to be good at writing and be creative in order to assist in selling a product. Of course, you can also be a journalist, an author, a blogger and so on.

3. **Are you analytical and a critical thinker?** Engineering is a great avenue to explore if you have these skills. Consulting is also an excellent role as you can go into different companies and recommend changes to their organizations.

4. **Do you like technology?** Are you innovative? With so much innovation and automation these days, this is a great field to be in.

5. **Do you like science and biology?** There are so many opportunities for people to become doctors, nurses, technicians or therapists, for example.

6. **Do you like to act and sing?** The entertainment field is a great place for those who have the talent, although it is not an easy profession to get into. If you have the patience and persistence, then this is the right career for you.

7. **Do you have the "gift of gab"?** Are you an extrovert and enjoy influencing others? Sales may be the right place for you. You must really like to talk to people to be in this role. You must be highly motivated to uncover people's needs and match them with a product or a service. This job can be a real rollercoaster.

8. **Do you like to read?** Are you passionate about the justice system? Perhaps you might want to consider becoming a lawyer. If you want to be a trial lawyer, you will need to be able to excel at public speaking. This career may require working very long hours, so this is something to think about as you assess your options.

9. **Are you good with your hands?** Do you like to fix things around the house? Having your own business as a contractor, a plumber or an electrician can be very lucrative.

10. **Do you like to help people?** Teachers, police, firefighters, or the military are great professions to be in to help others. These are tough careers because you put your life at risk every day.

11. **Are you a strategic thinker who has many creative ideas?** You may be entrepreneurial and could start you own business. I had been thinking about starting my own business for many years, but I just didn't have the guts to do it. I finally did it and it is one of the best things I could have done in my life.

12. **What environment do you thrive in?** This is an important point to consider when you are looking for a

career that you will be happy in. For example, the asset management industry is conservative. In addition to your skills, you could be judged on how you dress and how you wear your hair. If you like a more casual atmosphere you may want to consider going to a startup or a smaller firm.

These are just some areas that may interest you, but there are many more. It is okay if you do not know yet – that is why it is helpful to put the list together. Not everyone is suited for the corporate world. You may want to own your own business.

Once you think about the things that interest you, you also need to assess if you have the right skills. You may really like a certain career, but you may not have the right skill sets. For instance, if you think you want to be a lawyer, but you don't love to read or you do not like to speak in public, this may not be the right career for you.

While you are thinking about the things you like to do, you should also think about what skills you have. The important thing to think about is even if you don't have the right skills now, you can develop those skills over time. For example, my brother-in-law became a lawyer in his 30s. One of his issues was he didn't love to read. He ended up taking a speed-reading course and he went to law school. He became a very successful mediator.

I also had a chance to be a relationship manager in my career. A relationship manager manages client relationships for the firm. I did it for 1 year and I really liked it, but the problem was, I wasn't really the best person for the job. Sure, I did the role and was good, but I really was much better at being a manager. It took me some time to realize this, but I know now I made the right decision in the end.

ACTIONS YOU CAN TAKE:

- **Answer the questions above** to determine where your interests lie.
- **Keep a list of your interests and talents** every time you learn something new that you like, add it to your list. If you have a smart phone, you can easily create a list in your Notes app.
- **Take a career assessment test.** There are various sites that have free assessments. These tests are informal assessments that determine a person's work style, motivations, beliefs and aptitude. The results can help guide you towards a career that best fits your skills. They shouldn't be the only thing to use but can help you in your decisions in determining the right job for you.

CHAPTER 2

LANDING THE JOB OF
YOUR DREAMS

"Choose a job you love, and you will never have to work a day in your life."

Confucius

If you are just out of college or have recently left your job, you may be struggling to know where to begin your search for the job of your dreams. It is not always easy to do and it often can take six months to a year to find the right job, depending on your career choice or the market.

In the past, most people used a recruiter, which may have made the job search seem much easier. Recruiters worked for you, the individual, to find you the right job based on your skill set and your interests. Now it seems recruiters work increasingly on behalf of companies to fill open roles, rather than with the individual to find multiple opportunities. I was successful in the past using recruiters, but today there are many other ways to find a job, ranging from online hiring platforms to social media so it definitely helps to be flexible.

One of the most effective ways to secure a job today is to know or be connected with people at a company with the goal of eventually getting an interview. If you have been in an organization for many years, you may only know the people you work with. This will not help you in your broader job search. There are many networking opportunities that you can be involved in. Even during the COVID pandemic when we were all house bound, there were still virtual networking opportunities through platforms like Zoom or Google Meetup. You can find networking events on LinkedIn by joining groups in your industry.

The first thing to do (if you have not done so already) is to create a LinkedIn profile. LinkedIn has become my number one source for networking and job searching. I have met so many individuals through LinkedIn. It not only helps with job search, but it can also help those like me who are starting their own businesses.

The other great thing about LinkedIn is the online training that is available. It is training that may not be offered in your current organization, or, if you are not working, it is good to have this available at your fingertips to improve your skills. At the time of this writing, it cost about $350 a year, but it is well worth the money.

Research the companies that are in the area of what you want to do. It really helps to get an understanding of a company's culture so you can make an assessment of whether it is the right fit for you. It helps to speak with people who work at the company. I typically research on LinkedIn to see who works there and, if I know them, I send them a message to see if they have time to speak about the company.

Even if you do not know anyone at the company, it still does not hurt to reach out to someone who works there. I have met so many people who are willing to take time to speak to people and help them with their career. Many people have reached out to me directly as well, and I am always happy to speak with them.

ACTIONS YOU CAN TAKE:

- **Set up your LinkedIn profile** – Make sure it is professional including your experience and how you've made an impact in your role(s). Start connecting with all the people you know, and for those who might be directly related to your interest, message them or ask for an in-person or online meeting if you have meaningful questions to ask about their industry or role.
- **Join networking groups** in your industry so that you can start to get to know people outside your organization. See more on networking in Chapter 24.
- **Find a recruiter** who specializes in your industry.
- **Research companies** in your industry to get an understanding of their culture so you can determine if they are the right fit for you. You can use websites like Glassdoor which gives ratings and reviews from existing and former employees

CHAPTER 3

WHAT CAN YOU DO TO BE SUCCESSFUL IN THE JOB?

"Do what you can with all you have, wherever you are."

Theodore Roosevelt

You do not often just land the job of your dreams right away, and you often will not know at first whether it is the job of your dreams. As I look back on my career, I can see each of the jobs I was in as a steppingstone to where I am now, even if I did not see it at the time. Whether I was happy or not, I did learn a lot from every experience.

Today, I see many young people who do not want to start out at entry level. They seem to be bored right from the start. I get it – no one wants to do the boring stuff! My advice to them is to be patient and learn as much as they can where they are so they can begin to develop the foundational experience for a successful career.

Whether you are an assistant or in an analyst program, you are definitely going to have to do tasks that seem mundane but ultimately are important to the organization. While you may feel stuck with doing some of these tasks, it also can give you the time to network and meet people in your organization. Sign up for any networking groups the company has to offer, whether that is women's groups, Black and Hispanics, LGBTQ+ or others. This is the ideal time for you to learn as much as you can about the organization, your interests, your work style and the types of projects you would like to be involved in.

When I started at *1838* as a portfolio accountant, I did not know anything about the asset management industry. I was in a role where I was reconciling portfolios to the custodian information. This was a very mundane task, and today this is automated in most companies.

As I was performing this task, I made sure that I understood exactly what I was doing by asking a lot of questions. I even went to the portfolio managers to learn more about how the securities worked. That curiosity made me even more valuable to the company because it enabled an accurate work product, namely that the clients' portfolios were correct.

You can always link back what you are doing to your organization's clients. The function you are performing is providing value to the client. Remembering this gives you a greater sense of purpose in your role. It helps you to gain passion in what you are doing day to day.

You have a very unique opportunity when starting a new role at a firm…. you are given a chance to recreate yourself. You can leave all the misconceptions about yourself behind you and start fresh. I discovered this when I joined my latest company. No one knew me (maybe a few former colleagues from previous firms), and it provided the chance for me to start over. I have found this to be true whenever I started a new job.

When I was at MS, I dealt with many challenges. One of my biggest challenges was moving up the ranks within the company. I was promoted to vice president after being there over 10 years. I spent the next 10 years trying to get promoted to executive director. It never happened. When I left and went to another company, they did not have titles. This allowed me to look at the job a little differently.

Did I really need to have a certain job title to prove my worth? Absolutely not! Not having the title allowed me to perform my role without focusing on being promoted. It became an unimportant career goal.

This is when I learned my lesson – why was I so consumed with having that title? I thought having the title would make me successful. This couldn't be further from the truth. Doing what you love and helping others be successful, can make all the difference in your career. Success is subjective. It means different things to different people. If I had just done my job and focused on being the best that I could be, it would have made me a lot happier and relieved a lot of the stress I felt at the time.

ACTIONS YOU CAN TAKE:

- When you start a new job, do the following:
  - o **Learn as much as you can** about the role.
  - o **Get to know everyone** you work with and learn about what they do.
  - o **Join the company's networking groups**.

- **Remember that no task is too mundane** – Every function adds value to the organization's clients.
- **Do not focus on your title** – Just focus on doing the best job you can do.

CHAPTER 4

HOW TO DEAL WITH OFFICE POLITICS?

"In weak companies politics win, in strong companies, best ideas do."

Steve Jobs

I have seen office politics play out many times in my career. While they are a reality in most firms, there are other ways to become successful. Additionally, the increased corporate focus on inclusion and diversity in the workplace (see Chapter 14 for more details on Diversity and Inclusion) appears to be turning the tide on politics and putting the emphasis on more important success factors.

But what are office politics anyway? Office politics are the unwritten rules in a workplace. It is hard to put into words exactly what these are, but you will know when you find yourself in a situation in which office politics are being played out. It is typically something that appears to not be fair to others – someone gets something because of how they look, because they are friends with their manager and so on.

People often think that you cannot get ahead unless you play by the rules of office politics. I disagree with this – and I also would not want to get ahead by playing by these rules. Here are some examples of office politics I have experienced in the past and how I dealt with them without playing the game:

- **Example 1**: Many years ago, I worked for a boss who did not like women. Especially women who were smarter than he. He did not have a college degree, so it felt as though he was trying to compensate for that by being a bully. When I tried to be honest with him about the way he was managing, he called me insubordinate. I was up for a promotion that year, and he told me that my name was being pulled.

  How I handled it: I was devastated when my boss pulled my name out of the running because I had worked so hard, and I felt I really deserved the promotion. It did make me realize that I needed to leave this position, and so I ended up going to a different business unit within the same company. It was good to move to a different area because I got to learn different things, which only helped me grow in my career. I ended up leaving the company one year later and it was the one of best decisions I ever made. I never looked back! Sometimes you cannot do anything to change the situation and you must make a decision that is best for you. You can either stay and continue to do the best job you can do or you can leave to start something new.

- **Example 2**: There seems to always be one person in a team who gets picked for all the good projects or exposure to senior management. I had a person on my team a few years ago who was like this. She was very good at setting up meetings with senior management and letting them know how great she was. She would get a lot of accolades, but she was really not the person on the team who had the knowledge or did the hard work in getting the job done. This made others on the team feel that they weren't being treated fairly because they were doing good work, but not getting the same recognition that she was getting. **How I handled it:** I called attention to this to management, so they were aware of how it made others on the team feel. Slowly but surely, management began to understand that they needed to give others on the team a chance, too. They started giving other members of the team a chance to get exposure to senior management by putting them on high profile projects.

If you see something that is wrong, you need to speak up about it. Not everything is going to be resolved right away. You do have to be delicate in the way you handle the situation as you do not want to seem vindictive or petty. You can tell management, but then it is up to them to figure out how to handle it. Patience can be a virtue in these situations...it can sometimes take years for these situations to work out.

- **Example 3:** A few years ago, I was moved out of my position as head of a team. A woman who had been brought in as a business manager for the head of the department and had been in the position for a year, was then put in a position over me. I was then moved into a different position. They called it a promotion, but no one (including myself) saw it as such. It was not a job I had asked for, nor was it something I wanted to do. **How I handled it:** I was so unhappy about the situation, as I felt that I was being pushed out of a role I was passionate about – managing a team. I had taken the team from a back-office function to a key client partner. It had not been easy, and I certainly had not been perfect in everything I had done, but I was not ready to move to a different role. I did a lot of soul searching to understand why this had happened to me and I read a lot of books to see how I could move on. One book that really helped me was *Everything is Figureoutable* by Marie Forleo. It made me really think about the value that everyone brings and the many opportunities there are out there for all of us.

While I was still unhappy with the situation, I began to embrace the job. I learned as much as I could, and I began to see impactful results in the work I did. I also started to look at what I could change about my life that would make me happier. I got a certificate in coaching and started my own coaching business. I now write blogs monthly, and I coach clients. It is really what brought me to writing this book. I also took time to get training at work to help me grow in areas where I had opportunities. I now recognize why I may have been moved into this position. I did need to strengthen my leadership skills and learn ways to influence people to adapt to change.

The only real way to combat office politics is to be aware that they are happening and to use your voice. Let management know if you see something that you think is not fair and if you must, escalate to your HR department. You need to have evidence and you should be careful in how you approach the situation. Do not be combative. Be sure to take a professional approach so that you do not burn bridges along the way.

ACTIONS YOU CAN TAKE:

- **Pay attention to how office politics work** in your organization. This isn't easy to do, but you will discover in time who the players are in the organization. You need to be aware of this so you can avoid getting involved on the wrong side of the situation. Try to find a trusted colleague who can help you manage through.

- **Find** ways to cope with the situation. I was able to do this by reading self-help books. You may find talking to others may help too.
- **Check out your firm's Employee Assistance Program** if you need someone to speak to right away.
- **Try not to let your emotions get the best of you.** I know this is easier said than done, but if you take a step back from the situation, and think about it before reacting, your outcome will almost always be more successful. My daughter once told me "It's not what happens to you, but it is how you react to your situation."

CHAPTER 5

THE MICROMANAGER AND THE BULLY BOSS

"A bad job with a good boss is better than a good job with a bad boss."

Unknown

Where do I start? I have had so many different bosses in my career, and I remember having many micromanagers and, of course, my fair share of bully bosses. It is so important to have a good relationship with your manager/boss. It can sometimes determine your happiness in the role.

Here are the examples of each type and how to identify them.

The micromanager

Micromanagers are very easy to spot. They are the managers who love to control everything their employees do. They tend to suck the passion and joy out of their employees by controlling every aspect of their job. It can make employees feel as though they need to run and run fast!

Sometimes you cannot run because there may not be the right jobs to run to, and you must stay with the micromanager. The first step is identifying when you have a micromanager and how to handle them.

Here are the ways to spot the micromanager:

- They want to control everything their team does from end to end. They may even write emails for you to send. Yes, it is that frustrating!
- They may keep a running list of everything that is going on in their team. Everything from when you take vacation to making sure you dotted your i's and crossed your t's.
- They sometimes like to take credit for other people's work and fail to give their team members exposure to senior management. This does not allow for their employees to grow in their careers.
- They tend to be insecure, which is why they want to do everything, so no one looks better than they do. They want senior management to think that they are the ones who do everything to make the team great.

Here are some tips on how to handle micromanagers:

1. Keep a list of everything you do. This way, when they ask you what you have done or what the status is, you will have it handy.
2. You may want to copy them in on everything you do, so they know firsthand what you are working on. After doing this for some time, they may even ask you to stop copying them in because they cannot keep track of all the emails. This is a good thing.
3. Speak to them about your frustrations. It can help the manager to understand that what they are doing is not

helping you and may even lead to your leaving your position. They might begin to realize that they need to change their leadership style.

4. Try not to let this get you down, especially if you cannot move to another position. Do not let their behavior reflect on your work. If you are working hard and adding value, you will begin to get noticed by the right people. Keep working hard until you are able to move to another team or another job outside the firm.

The bully boss

I have had two bully bosses in my career. It was challenging to work with them. It was scary and they were definitely the most stressful times I have had in my career.

Here are the ways to spot the bully boss:

- Like micromanagers, they tend to be insecure. They do not like anyone to show them up.
- They do not like people on their teams who are well liked by senior management.
- Some keep a list of best practices on how you should deal with them – oh yes! I had a boss who kept a list. It even had on it "no gum chewing or clicking your pen during meetings".
- They may have deadlines on when they want presentations before meetings and if they do not receive it at the exact time, they chastise you via email. Whenever you get an email in all caps, they are yelling at you. (Yes, this did happen to me!)
- They can be aggressive, put you down in front of others and have unreasonable demands.

- They tell others that you are incompetent and thereby can ruin your reputation.

Bully bosses are the worst types of managers to deal with. I would suggest the following to deal with a bully:

1. Make sure you have a weekly catch-up meeting with them to go through your priorities with a status for each item.
2. Try to find out the best way to communicate with them. If they have a list of best practices, make sure to read it. You do not have to follow it, but you should be aware of them.
3. Find a mentor or a career coach. They can assist you in how to deal with the situations you are facing with your boss.
4. If it gets really bad, contact your Employee Assistance Program. This is a safe way to discuss the issues with no repercussions. They will not tell your manager. This may be safer than going to HR. While you may think HR is there for the employee, most are required to give updates to your manager. This happened to me, and my manager told me never go to HR again.
5. If all else fails, it is time to look for another job. No job is worth putting up with a bully and wreaking havoc on your health.

I had a bad experience many years ago with a passive aggressive manager and her manager, who was a bully. My career coach said it was like having an abusive father with a mother who looked the other way. It was so true. My immediate boss did nothing and she would yell at me for things the bully told her about me.

I went to HR, and it did not end too well. My boss ended up hearing about it and treated me horribly for the next few months.

My stress level was through the roof. I was managing a large team and trying to remain calm for them. I did not want them to know that my boss and her boss were so tough. I ended up resigning, but at the same time the bully went on a leave of absence, and I was asked to stay.

Sometimes situations end up working out for you in the end. This is why it is so important to be your best self, go out and do the best that you can, and in the end, things just may end up working out in your best interest whether it is leaving the firm or staying with a new opportunity!

ACTIONS YOU CAN TAKE:

- **Get to know your manager's style** and learn how they like to be communicated with. You may need to develop an email template for them so that you include the details they want to see.
- **Find ways to build your relationship with your manager** – ask them if they would like to go to lunch. Going outside the office helps to build a personal relationship with them as well.
- **Find a mentor or a career coach** to help you manage the relationship with your boss if you find yourself in any difficult situations. I could never have dealt with my situation without my career coach. She made all the difference in my situation.

CHAPTER 6

ARE YOU GETTING THE ACKNOWLEDGEMENT FOR THE WORK YOU ARE DOING?

"Leaders don't look for recognition from others, leaders look for others to recognize."

Simon Sinek

Have you ever worked really hard on something and not received the recognition you felt you were deserved? Do you feel you keep getting overlooked by management? This happens frequently in the corporate world, and it can make employees very unhappy. It is a shame that companies do not recognize this as one of the key reasons top talent leaves their firms.

It can be very challenging when you feel like you are not getting recognized for the work you are doing. Maybe you think your boss does not like you, and you do not know where to turn.

What can you do if you feel you are not getting recognized? Here are a few suggestions:

1. **Continue to work hard** – Most people say you cannot just work hard to be successful. I disagree. Hard workers

are the most valuable employees. They may keep their heads down and work, but they get shit done! Keep doing the best job you can. You will get noticed by the right people. Even if you feel you are not being recognized, you are. The right people will notice in time.

2. **Use your voice** – Sometimes hard workers are too busy to promote what they are doing. Make the time to let management know what you are doing and tell them you want to be included in the meetings that allow you to present the work you have done. Think about ways you can tell your story. You can put together a PowerPoint slide on your accomplishments with focus areas for the remainder of the year. Share this with your manager at your next one on one meeting. You should have at least a biweekly meeting with your manager to share this information with them. If you do not, ask them about scheduling one.

3. **Meet with senior management** – If your manager is not giving you the opportunity, you can set up your own meetings with senior management. You do not have to tiptoe around your manager. Hierarchical structures do not mean you cannot meet with the boss's boss! Send an email first to the senior manager letting them know that you would like to meet with them and explain why. For example, you can say you want to learn more about the priorities for the year or you are interested in learning about their career journey. Senior managers may be busy, but they will find time to help keep talent in their organizations.

4. **Get a mentor** – It really helps to talk to someone in the company who is not your manager or has control over your work. They can give you constructive feedback that your manager may not be giving to you. Sometimes

you need someone to tell you the real reason you are not being promoted or why you are not being given those high-profile projects.

Do not stay in a position where you are not recognized for the work you are doing. If you really feel unhappy, it may be time to look for another position, either within the company or outside.

ACTIONS YOU CAN TAKE:

- **Work hard** – Keep doing the best work you can do. Do not let a negative culture get the best of you......and leverage positive cultures to maximize your opportunities.
- **Use your voice** – Tell your story – it may mean doing a presentation on your accomplishments and focus areas for the year. If you do not have a one-on-one meeting with your manager, make sure you set that up with them at least biweekly.
- **Change your situation** – If the situation does not get better, consider looking for another position.
- **Do not let anyone steal your power away** – Keep going to work with your head held high and remember the value you bring to the organization. More on this in Chapter 24.

CHAPTER 7

WHAT DO I NEED TO DO TO GET PROMOTED?

"Some people want it to happen, some wish it would happen, others make it happen."

Michael Jordan

If you find that you are not getting ahead in your current position, it is time to do a self-assessment of your performance. Sometimes people think they are doing all the right things to get ahead, and they still are not getting promoted. They are thinking, "This isn't fair. Why is everyone else getting promoted, but I'm stuck on ground 1?" I know, because I have been there many times. I did not always do the right things to understand why I was stuck. Maybe I was afraid to hear things that I already knew deep inside.

Here are some of my suggestions for getting on the right path for a promotion:

1. **Be visible** – Show people the value you add. Let management know what you are working on that has added value to the team and the firm. Providing a weekly or biweekly update is helpful.

2. **Be present in meetings** – Do not just sit on the side and take notes. Be engaged and ask questions. Always go to the meeting in person rather than staying at your desk. Find time to prepare for meetings ahead of time so that you can ask questions.

3. **Network** – Do not stay at your desk all day. Make sure you build relationships up and down the organization. Grab a quick coffee with a colleague or schedule a 1:1 with a senior manager. You can do this even when working remotely. Set up zoom calls with your colleagues. More on this in Chapter 23.

4. **If you do not ask, the answer will always be NO** – If management does not know what you want in your career, they cannot help you. Make sure your manager is aware of how you would like to progress in your career.

5. **The right attitude matters** – Be sure that you keep a positive attitude even in challenging times. Complaining does not help but providing innovative ideas or solutions to help a team move in the right direction can. At times, when you are frustrated about your situation at work, your attitude can change for the worse. This is not good because now you are being perceived as having a bad attitude. You must turn that attitude around quickly because it will hurt your chances for a promotion later.

6. **Ask for feedback** –At a previous company, I consistently received good reviews, but did not get promoted. It was frustrating, but I never asked for additional feedback. Now I always ask because if you are getting good reviews and not getting promoted something is not right. They aren't giving you direct feedback to help you grow in your position. This happened when I went for a position and was initially told, "No, because I need you where you are". I thought this was such a lame response. I stewed over it

a bit and then went back to ask for additional feedback. This is when I got the truth: I was told that I needed to develop my strategic leadership skills.

7. **Develop your skills** – While you do not necessarily need to agree with the feedback given, if you keep hearing the same things over and over, you may need to realize that you have an issue in that area. I took the feedback about my strategic leadership skills and decided to take a class. I enrolled in an "Executive Presence and Persuasive Leadership" program at Wharton. I found it to be so enlightening, and I learned things that I can now apply to my job. I will go into more details in Chapter 10 on Executive Presence and Chapter 11 on Developing Your Skills.

It is not always easy to get promoted, even when you think you deserve it. One of the things you can do to get through it is act as the leader you want to be. Once you act the part, the next step may not be as far away as you think!

ACTIONS YOU CAN TAKE:

- **Be visible** – Let management know what you are doing. Tell your story and ask for what you want in your career.
- **Ask for feedback** – After every presentation or communication with senior management, ask what went well and what you could have done better. Apply those learnings in your next situation with them to show progress.
- **Develop your skills** – Start building a list of skills you want to develop (more on this in Chapter 11).

CHAPTER 8

ARE YOU HAPPY IN YOUR CURRENT JOB?

"Success is liking yourself, liking what you do and liking how you do it."

Maya Angelou

Are you happy in your job? I must ask myself this question a lot because the answer can be very different depending on the day. I feel my emotions about work change constantly. I can have days when I feel good about the job I do and days when I feel unhappy about the work. I often must readjust my mindset and focus on things I can control.

Being passionate about what you do usually helps in finding happiness in your job. Sometimes you may not be passionate about your current job, but you can still find happiness.

These are some things I have learned to do when feeling unhappy with my job:

1. **List your accomplishments or "wins"** – Write down all the areas where you have added value in your current role. This will help you to think differently about your

role and consider what your passion is. Creating a journal or list of your wins each day will help you start to understand how you add value to your organization.

2. **Do not complain** – I find that, when I complain about something, it makes me feel worse. Instead, I try to communicate a solution to make things better.

3. **Focus on the positive** – There are always going to be things you do not like about your job, but if you want to be happier, focus on the good things. Maybe it is your colleague who has become a friend, or you have a great manager – these things are important!

4. **Focus on things you can control** – I love to help others be successful. When I am not happy with work, I focus on things I can do to help others. Maybe create a training program, share interesting articles or set up a catch up with a colleague.

Whenever I get into a funk about my personal life or career, I look for self-help books or classes that can guide me in the right direction.. When I was moved to a position that I was not happy about (see Chapter 4), I started reading Shirzad Chamine's book *Positive Intelligence* and took his mental fitness training for coaches a few years ago. Shirzad speaks about the Positive Intelligence Quotient (PQ), which is the "percentage of time your mind acts as your friend rather than as your enemy." Shirzad explains that we can increase our PQ in order to achieve higher performance, greater happiness and less stress (you can learn more about Positive Intelligence and take your PQ assessment at this link: https://upliftcareercoaching.com/new-positive-intelligence).

In his teachings, Shirzad talks about "Saboteurs". Saboteurs are the negative voices in our head that tell us that we are not good enough and that others are not good enough, which causes negative emotions. The "Judge" is the Master Saboteur. The Judge affects everyone. It is the one that beats you up repeatedly over your mistakes and shortcomings. In order to get rid of the Judge, we must name it and recognize when we are listening to it. We do this through PQ repetitions, which build up our mental muscles in order to get rid of our Saboteurs.

The "Sage" is our positive muscle. It gives us gifts to change how we think about a negative situation or event. You can look at the situation or event as an opportunity to learn from it. For example, the COVID pandemic was a bad time for all of us, but we can look at it in a different way; for example, it gave some people more time with their families.

During my mental fitness training, Shirzad also told us the story of Christopher Reeve which really resonated with me. Christopher Reeve was a famous actor who starred in the first Superman movie in 1978. In 1995, Christopher became paralyzed from the neck down and was unable to breathe on his own without a ventilator after he was thrown from his horse. Christopher told his wife then, "maybe we should let me go."

While Christopher was not happy with his situation, he didn't want to give up on life and decided that he wanted to use what happened to him as an opportunity to help others. He started to use his celebrity to put a focus on spinal cord injuries. He helped support disability legislation and he dedicated the rest of his life on improving the quality of life for people with disabilities. He eventually co-founded the "Christopher Reeve Foundation". The foundation has given over $65 million to research. According to UC Irvine, "Christopher did more to promote research on spinal cord injury than any other person before or since."

This was a lightbulb moment for me. It made me think, how could I be so unhappy when a person who had so much suffering was able to turn that around to help others. This made me realize that I wanted to do the same thing.

Using Shirzad's teachings and mental fitness application, I learned to do two-minute PQ meditations that can help change your mindset. They are as simple as closing your eyes and listening to the train or the cars, or you can focus for two minutes on the beauty of an object, like a flower or a painting.

This really helped me to change my mindset during frustrating moments at work. By taking a time out and doing a meditation, you can leave the frustrations behind and begin to focus on another task. It is okay to get upset about an issue, but you do not want to stay there too long. In the past, I could spend my whole day being upset over one little issue.

I also think about the things that make me happy about the job. I love the people I work with, so I focus on spending time with them, thinking about ways I can help them, especially the younger colleagues. Doing these things often makes me feel better about the job.

Have you ever heard the quote "Act like the leader you wish you had"? I do this often and I think about the fact that I do not need a title to be the leader. I have the skills to take the lead, so I just do it.

There are always going to be times when others are more successful than you, and you may think it is unfair. And it may be unfair. But you cannot dwell on this. Remember, you do not have to compare your life to others. If they do well, be happy for them. You can still be successful. Focus on your opportunities and the things that you like to do. If you keep your focus on yourself, it will only help you be successful.

ACTIONS YOU CAN TAKE:

- **Check your wins** – If you are feeling unhappy about your job, think about those things that you like about it. Start by listing your accomplishments.
- **Do not complain to your coworkers** – This will only make you feel worse. Be constructive and think about ways you can help your coworkers.
- **Focus on yourself** – Your career shouldn't be your main focus in your life. Think about those things that you can do in your personal life. Finding a new hobby can help take your mind off your career.

CHAPTER 9

WHAT IF YOU'RE NOT IN THE RIGHT JOB?

"The only person you are destined to become is the person you decide to be."

Ralph Waldo Emerson

Sometimes, it is hard to figure out whether you are in the right job and if your job is making you happy. In Chapter 8, I talked about the things you can do to make you happier in your job. Now I want to focus on whether you think you are in the right job. Here are some questions you can ask yourself to determine whether you are:

- **Do you have the right skills for your current position?** Sometimes people are put into roles for which they do not have the right skills or experience. For example, people who are good at their day-to-day functions may be promoted to a manager position without any experience or training. The person may not be happy with their role, and the people they manage may be unhappy too.

- **Are you passionate about what you are doing?** Do you wake up every morning thinking that you cannot wait to tackle a particular problem to get your team to the next level? Passion is important because it helps you to be productive.

- **Do you see career progression in the future?** Does senior management know who you are and what you are doing? Does your current job offer the opportunity to engage with senior managers? This is important if you want to get ahead in your career.
- **Do you feel valued for the work you are doing?** Feeling valued helps fuel passion, which fuels productivity. If you do not feel valued, you most likely are not going to be happy or feel passionate about what you are doing.
- **Are you in the right work environment?** We have all heard of toxic work environments. If you are in one, it can be damaging to your emotional health (see Chapters 12 and 13).

These are just a few questions that you can ask yourself to determine whether you are in the right job or whether it is time for a change. Making a career change can be difficult. Sometimes people feel safe where they are because they have been at a company for many years. I know; I was in this predicament years ago. I stayed at a company because I had worked there for a long time and I had young kids, so going to a new company felt scary. I thought, "What if it doesn't work out?" I know now that I should have asked myself, "What if it does work out?"

As I get older, I want to enjoy my life and my career, so I think about being happy in all areas of my life. If I am not happy, I am going to let people know and do something about it to change the situation for the better. It is not always easy to speak up or make a change, but it is your life, so it is something you should be doing. Do not stay where you feel you do not belong.

Times can be challenging, and it may not be the easiest time to look for a new position, but there is always time to put a plan together for your future. Whether it is looking at new opportunities or learning something new, today is always a good time to start.

ACTIONS YOU CAN TAKE:

- **Research yourself and your job** – Write a pros and cons list about your job. If you have more cons than pros, it may be time to look for another job.
- **Talk to your mentor or a career coach** – It helps to talk to someone besides your manager and have them work with you and guide you to what you could be doing differently to find a role were you will be a better fit.

CHAPTER 10

DO YOU HAVE EXECUTIVE PRESENCE?

"Leadership is about making others better as a result of your presence and making sure that impact lasts in your absence."

Sheryl Sandberg

As I am writing this chapter, I have just received a certificate from Wharton in their program "Executive Presence and Persuasive Leadership". A few years ago, I was told by my then manager that I needed to develop my executive presence. I was taken aback by this. I had always taken presentation skills classes and executive presence training in the past, so I thought my skills were ok.

She told me that senior managers didn't see me as a leader, and I need to be clearer and more concise in my messaging to them in meetings. I was really thrown for a loop on this. I even told her that I'm getting older, and I don't think I need to spend time developing this skill. I thought I am myself and if people don't like it, that is their problem.

Boy was I wrong! I didn't want to hear the feedback and my manager was really trying to help me. Even though, I didn't believe her, I did try to take steps to improve my presentation and communication skills.

I do believe it was my confidence that was impacting my skills. I do tend to get intimated by senior managers especially those that aren't friendly (aka bullies!). I tend to let this get into my head right before a big meeting or presentation.

When my then-manager announced her retirement, I was sad because she was one of the best managers I had ever had. I had learned so much from her. But I also looked at this as an opportunity for the team and for me.

While I knew that her boss did not see me as a senior leader, I was still going to ask for the role. I put together a proposal of how I thought the organization should be structured and I set up a meeting with the boss. I presented the proposal and told her why I was the right person for the job. She liked the proposal but told me that they were interviewing a few external and internal people and she would get back to me in a few weeks.

A few weeks later she called me into her office to tell me that she was not going to give me the position. She told me that she needed me in my current position. I did not show my disappointment but thanked her for her time and left. After thinking about the message, she gave me, I knew there had to be more to it. If I was valuable in the role I was in, why would I not be given a chance to be promoted? I needed to find out from her exactly why she was not giving me the chance. I went back to her, and she explained that I needed to develop my strategic leadership skills and persuasive communication to senior management.

I researched multiple programs and even interviewed a career coach but, in the end, decided that the Wharton Executive Presence and Persuasive Leadership program was the best choice for me. I was able to learn so much about leadership and persuasive communication.

Here are some of the takeaways from the course:

- Learn the most important **leadership principles** including:

  o Articulate a vision – communicate what your vision is for the team or project. What do you expect to achieve?

  o Think and Act Strategically - build a strategic plan to achieve your vision

  o Communicate Persuasively – use storytelling

  o Motivate the troops – build on your teams' unique strengths

  o Embrace the Front Lines – empower others by delegating authority

  o Build leadership in others – think about how you can make other leaders instead of followers

  o Manage relations – build close ties with the people you work with

  o Build a diverse team – when you bring in others with diverse skills and talents, you create an innovative team

- Use **storytelling** for persuasive communication.

  o A great example of this was Mr. Rogers testifying in Congress in 1969 about the need for budget for public television that his show was on at the time. If you are too young to know about Mr. Rogers, he was my favorite TV educational program when I was 5 years old. It was like Sesame Street. He taught children how each of us is unique and he liked us just the way we are. Mr. Rogers used storytelling to persuade Congress not to take away the budget for public television. He ended up being so persuasive that the lead senator who was tough in the beginning began to have tears in his eyes by the end. Mr. Rogers ended up getting double the budget rather than Congress taking the money away. See the YouTube video here to learn more - https://youtu.be/fKy7ljRr0AA

- Learn the **Persuasive Framework** of Logos, Pathos and Ethos -

  o **Logos** – means to be logical – have the right data points to boost your story. For example, if you are trying to get more headcount for your team, you need to show the volume of work that your team is doing in order to persuade management.
  o **Pathos** – means to appeal to emotions – This is what Mr. Rogers used in his appeal to congress for more money for public television.
  o **Ethos** – means to be credible – you need to be able to tell your story of why you are credible. Tell why you are the subject matter expert on this topic.

- **Network** inside and outside of the organization. See Chapter 23 for more on networking.
- Create **SMART (Specific, measurable, achievable, relevant, and time-bound) goals** to apply and develop your skills. For example, if you want to network more, create a list of the people you want to meet with and set target dates for setting up those meetings. SMART goals help keep you on track so that you can keep the promise to yourself to achieve them.

- **What is your vision?** If you lead a large team, articulate a vision for it – where is the team headed and how will it get there?

- **Be empathetic** – Everyone is facing challenges that we know nothing about. By listening and providing guidance to people, you can help them be successful.

- **Be present** – When you attend meetings, ensure you prepare beforehand, listen during the meeting and ask questions to learn more. You can also add your ideas or opinions.

- **Pause** – If you become frustrated in a meeting, do not bring your frustration to the next meeting. Pause and reframe your mindset (use the PQ meditations – see Chapter 6).

- **Ask for feedback** – Whether you are a manager or individual contributor, it is always helpful to ask for feedback. You do not have to take everything on board but make a note of themes you continue to hear over and over.

- **Learn** – You are never too old to learn a new skill. See Chapter 11 on Developing your skills.

- **Practice, practice, practice** – If you want to be a speaker, join a club or find speaking events where you can practice your skills. Toastmasters is a great club to perfect your presentation skills. I was part of this club for many years and learned to stop using "ums" and "ahs" after each sentence. I still do it, but not as much as I did.

- **Be authentic** – You do not have to change who you are to exude executive presence. You can be yourself but add a little confidence to that. Do not let someone's title scare you (see also Chapter 16).

One of the other important things that resonated with me from the program was learning about having the right mindset and going beyond "just world" thinking. Just world thinking is when you believe if you work hard, you should be rewarded and if you don't work hard, you should be punished.. This is not how real life works. You can't just sit at your desk all day and work hard and think this is all you need to do to been seen as a leader. You need to think about how the hard work you are doing will add value to your clients, your team, and your firm. Think about how you can make a real impact.

While I have learned a lot about executive presence, managers can use this as a reason for not promoting employees. It mostly impacts women and diverse individuals, which is why you need to be careful if your manager tells you this. You do not have to listen to everyone's opinion of you, even if it is your manager's. The best thing to do is get feedback from reliable colleagues including those senior to you, beside you and those in junior positions. This will give you constructive feedback that can help you develop your skills and understand the main themes that are coming out from the feedback. If executive presence is one of them, then it may be time to look at how you can develop these skills.

ACTIONS YOU CAN TAKE:

- **Practice, practice, practice** – I cannot say this enough, but the more you practice, the better your skills will get. Keep going to those meetings and volunteer to present.
- **Do not take it personally** – Do not take feedback personally. But if you keep hearing the same themes, it is time to develop your skills.
- **Keep up your confidence** – Do not let rejection get in the way of your confidence. Keep talking positively to yourself about how good you are and think about all the value you bring to your organization.

- **Do one thing each week to improve** – For example, write an email to a senior manager that you are intimidated by to build your relationship with them or set up a meeting with another senior person you admire to ask them how they became successful. Do something each day that scares you. The more you do it, the better you will become!

CHAPTER 11

YOU ARE NEVER TOO OLD TO DEVELOP YOUR SKILLS

"Live as if you were to die tomorrow. Learn as if you were to live forever."

Mahatma Gandhi

Most firms will have a mid-year and an annual review where your manager will review your strengths and opportunities to develop your skills. There has been some debate as to whether these are helpful to employees. I would say they are helpful if they are done correctly.

In most firms, a 360-feedback review is performed, which allows the employees to select a range of colleagues from all levels of the organization to give feedback. What I have found is that these reviews are not always constructive, because people do not usually want to say anything negative about their colleagues. While I understand this, it does not help anyone if the feedback is not honest and constructive.

The manager takes this feedback and a self-review from the employee and puts together the review. Once they complete this, they have a conversation with the employee to discuss. As a manager, I have found these can be good conversations with the employee because I have been giving them feedback all through the year about where they can improve. I do not put anything in the review that has not been discussed with them previously.

As an employee, I have found that the reviews are sometimes filled with surprises, and I often do not agree with everything that is said. I have seen managers who are afraid to tell you something during the year and then they put it in the review. This is not fair as it does not give the employee the chance to improve during the year.

While I may not always agree with the feedback, I do try to look at the opportunities identified and see where I can improve. I would suggest that if you are unhappy with your feedback, speak to your manager to understand and get more details.

Once you put together the list of development opportunities, add in what your goals are to make improvements in these areas. Review the list with your manager so they understand you are committed to making improvements.

I always go to books or take training classes to work on my improvements. Most firms have training course to help, but you may have to look outside. Many universities offer great online certification programs, especially for those who want to move into a management position in the future.

Here are some of my favorite authors and books that I have read over the years that have helped me improve my skills:

- Simon Sinek – *Start with Why; Leaders Eat Last; The Infinite Game*
- Brene Brown – *Dare to Lead*
- Stephen Covey – *The 7 Habits of Highly Effective People*

- Marie Forleo – *Everything is Figureoutable*
- Mel Robbins – *The 5 Second Rule; The High 5 Habit*
- Anthony Robbins – *Re-Awaken the Giant Within*
- Elle Russ – *Confident as Fu*k*
- Ray Dalio – *Principles*
- Mark Manson – *The Subtle Art of Not Giving a F*ck*
- Susan Jeffers – *Feel the Fear and Do It Anyway*

These books have helped me to overcome issues that I was facing in the workplace. Whenever I am facing problems in my personal life or my career, I look for answers in books. As I mentioned previously, I read *Everything is Figureoutable* after I was moved into a different position. It helped me figure out how to move forward.

I read *Dare to Lead* when I was trying to figure out to how to be brave and face uncertainty head on while managing a large team. I ended up giving a copy to my management team so that we could learn together and also learn how to teach our teams the same.

When I was facing anxiety in my life, I picked up Mel Robbins' book, *The Five Second Rule*. Mel created this rule so that she could act on her goals instantly by counting down 5, 4, 3, 2, 1. It helped her get out of bed in the morning. It helped me learn to push myself to do things that I normally wouldn't do.

One of the first books I read early on in my career was *Feel the Fear and Do It Anyway*. I faced fear in my personal life and my career in my early twenties. I didn't know where to turn and this book helped me face my fears. I will never forget it!

If you need to make a change in your life, books can help give you a push. I find online training courses have also been helpful. Some companies offer reimbursement programs for you to take courses. As I mentioned, I loved the Wharton Executive Presence

Program and now I'm looking for my next online training on strategic leadership. If you want to develop your skills, there is a whole world of resources out there.

ACTIONS YOU CAN TAKE:

- **Create a list** – Put a list together of your development areas. These may come from your annual review or feedback that you receive from your manager and/or colleagues.
- **Write SMART goals** – Think about what you will need to do to develop these skills. Writing these down will help you do the things that you need to do to meet your goals.
- **Read a book** – Select one of the books listed above or another book of your choice that you think may help you along your career journey.

CHAPTER 12

DEALING WITH A TOXIC WORK ENVIRONMENT

"Everything negative – pressure, challenges – is all an opportunity for me to rise."

Kobe Bryant

Working in a toxic work environment can be damaging to your health. SHRM reported that the cost of turnover due to toxic workplaces has been over $223 billion over the past five years. One out of five workers have left their job due to toxic workplaces in the last five years, and six out of ten say they left because of their manager.

If you do find yourself in this type of environment, you want to be sure you have the right toolkit to handle the situation. I have been in a few toxic environments during my career, and it has been challenging. My time working with the bully boss I described in Chapter 5 was the most challenging in my career. There is not always an easy answer in how to deal with them, but here are some examples of difficult situations I have been in and how I have handled them.

- **Example 1:** I worked in a group that was perceived as a great team, but I found it to be a toxic environment. The head of the group was a bit of a bully and there was favoritism across the team. It reminded me of being in high school, with the popular people and the not-so-popular people. If you failed to be on the popular team, your career was going nowhere fast. This was a challenging environment, and it was difficult to determine how to handle it.

  How I handled it: I really did not know how to handle it effectively and I did not have many people to turn to because it was a very political environment. I had the choice between staying quiet and just getting my work done or saying something to change the situation.

  I identified a mentor and worked with her to understand what I could do about the situation. She was helpful as she gave me different options I could take in the situation.

  I finally realized that I couldn't change the situation and I either needed to get onboard with it or I needed to find another position. I also made the choice to focus on the positive. I loved the people I worked with, and I wanted to focus on helping them be successful. By doing this and not focusing on the toxic situation, it changed my mindset for the best. I became happier both at work and in my personal life.

  This may not always be the right way to handle a situation like this but having a coach or a mentor to talk it out with can help tremendously.

- **Example 2:** Many years ago, we had a woman in our team who was toxic. She was very good at her job and was well liked by the internal stakeholders that our team worked with. She was also well liked by senior management.

While management liked her, her colleagues on the team did not. As an individual performer, she was self-absorbed, condescending and not a team player. She was also passive-aggressive. When in meetings with the team, she would "humble brag". For example, she would say something to the effect of "I'm sorry I cannot attend the team training, but I will be presenting to the CEO at the same time" or "The CEO and I discussed that our team needs to be better in performing this process". This made others on the team feel as though they were not as important as she was and that she somehow had an "in" with senior management. She ended up becoming a manager which caused considerable angst among the team. They could not believe that this person could be promoted like this. They did not realize that, although she was not good at managing down or across, she was very good at managing up.

How I handled it: I spoke to my manager at the time about the behavior. This was before the individual got promoted. I thought being proactive and speaking to my manager would be the best course of action, but it did not work out well because this was a political environment, and the individual could not be touched. I began to stay quiet about the behavior and tried to ignore it.

My team members and other managers continued to complain about the behavior. It annoyed me as well, but I really did not know what I could do about it. It seemed that this was a protected person in the organization. I sent my manager an email about the situation and told her that this person needed to be held accountable for what she was doing, or it would destroy the morale of the team.

I may not have been able to change the situation in these two examples, but by speaking up about the issues, I made management aware that morale was affected. Situations do not always change overnight, and sometimes managers only start to listen when people start to leave the firm. Using your voice is the most important thing you can do. It may not help in every situation, but do not stay quiet.

ACTIONS YOU CAN TAKE:

- **Talk to the individual** whom you see exhibiting toxic behavior. This may be hard but letting them know that what you witnessed was inappropriate should be the first step. I always find giving the person the direct feedback before going to their manager is helpful. People are not always self-aware in how they are behaving. Once you give the direct feedback, it can help them realize the way they are behaving has a bad effect on morale.
- **Talk to your manager** - If after you give this feedback to the individual and the behavior does not change, it may be time to speak with your manager on how to handle.
- **Escalate to senior management** if your manager is not taking any action on the situation.

CHAPTER 13

MANAGING STRESS AND ANXIETY IN THE WORKPLACE

"The greatest weapon against stress is our ability to choose one thought over another."

William James

Mental health awareness is becoming even more important, especially given the many crises' we have had to deal with over past few years. It is time for all of us to be more aware of the impact of mental health issues on our society. I hear more and more young people who are affected by this. If you are feeling this way, please reach out to a mental health professional so they can help.

Dealing with stress and anxiety while working can be a challenge. I thought it would be helpful to share some tips on how I have overcome challenges with stress and anxiety in the workplace. Simple steps you take today can help you manage how you deal with these issues in the workplace and your personal life down the line.

As more awareness of mental health issues are being raised, more companies are providing support to employees. One tool that is used in some corporations for employees is meQuilibrium. This app allows employees to manage their stress levels and has activities that people can do to relieve stress. You can learn more about it at this link: https://www.mequilibrium.com.

Here are some other steps I have taken that may help you too if you are feeling stress or anxiety at work:

1. **Meditate** – Initially, I did not find this very useful, but then I made myself try it over time and found it does work. It is so helpful when you are feeling stressed. You can just pause what you are doing and refocus your mindset. (See Chapter 8).

2. **Take a walk** – If you are feeling emotional, do not stay at your desk. Get up and take a walk. It helps you get your mind off the issue you are dealing with at the moment. You may even find that you will come up with solutions because you are freeing your mind of worry or stress.

3. **Listen to music** – Music can really help to take your mind off your troubles. You can sing or dance to make yourself happier. When I am anxious before a big meeting or presentation, I listen to a song that is powerful, like Lady Gaga's "Stupid Love". If you sing or dance it out, it can really help relieve your nervous energy. Try it – I guarantee it works!

4. **Lose yourself in creativity** – This is not always easy to do in the workplace, but if you can, take some time out of your workday to be creative. Maybe it is working on a presentation or doing a craft, like painting, ceramics, pottery, and so on. Even doing something like this for just 30 minutes can help relieve stress. Add time for yourself to schedule these activities.

Doing these things does not mean you will never feel stress or anxiety again, but they are steps you can take so you do not stay in that mindset for too long. However, if doing these things does not help you, it may be time to investigate your organization's Employee Assistance Program. This is a program that can help you through your problems anonymously. Some programs give you a certain amount of free counseling sessions and then you can continue afterwards if you choose to do so. It is helpful to be able to talk through issues with a third party who knows nothing about you.

Make sure you spend time on your mental fitness, not just physical fitness. Doing so will help in all aspects of your life, allowing you to enjoy what you are doing rather than spending the time stressing.

ACTIONS YOU CAN TAKE:

- **Find a mental fitness plan** to help you cope.
- **Breathe** – Whenever in a situation that makes you upset, take time to breathe. Inhale through your nose and exhale through your mouth.
- **Take a walk** – I try to not let anyone see me get upset at work, so when I feel it coming, I take a walk around the block until I feel good enough to come back.
- **Find a hobby** outside of work to help you be creative and take your mind off what is stressing you. I have done watercolor painting, gardening, crocheting, baking and reading. I am still looking at other hobbies I can try. I want to learn tennis and golf next.

CHAPTER 14

DIVERSITY, INCLUSION AND EQUITY IN THE WORKPLACE

"An individual has not started living until he can rise above the narrow confines of his individualist concerns to the broader concerns of all humanity."
Martin Luther King, Jr.

Diversity, inclusion and equity, also known as DE&I, has recently become a more important topic in most firms across the United States, but it actually started in the mid-1960s during the Civil Rights Movement. It followed the equal employment laws and affirmative action.

In 2020, the death of George Floyd at the hands of a police officer increased DE&I programs at many corporations. People are more aware of the issues, and it is talked about more than ever before. Some firms even include this in performance reviews.

While increased awareness has been positive, many companies still have a long journey ahead to make notable progress. We talk about what is right and wrong in these programs, but I often do not see it in the day-to-day work. For example, there is still a gap in pay between men and women. In 2023, women made 77 cents to every dollar that men earn. This had not budged in over 20 years (see https://19thnews.org/2023/03/equal-pay-day-2023-charts-gender-pay-gap). It is even worse for diverse individuals, including LGBTQIA+, Black, Asian Pacific and Latino workers. Here is a table showing wages as compared to white men:

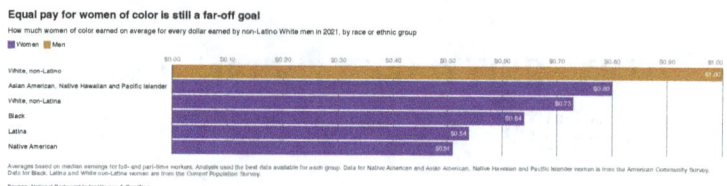

These statistics are not intended to scare you. However, if you are a diverse individual, it could be a challenging road and there are steps you need to take to help you get through these challenges.

Everyone is accountable for practicing diversity, inclusion and equity in everything we do. Every one of us is diverse. It is not only race, gender and sexual orientation. There are other diversities such as learning disabilities, sickness, religion and many others.

Here are ways to learn about and handle diversity in the workplace:

- **Learn about others and their cultures**. Learn how others want to be treated. There are many books available to increase your awareness and can help you direct conversations you can have with your colleagues about their culture.
- **Speak up about microaggressions or bias** that you see in your workplace. It can be scary to speak up, but you must do it in order to help others who may not speak up and ultimately to change the culture of the firm. If you feel frightened to do so, there are ways you can do

it anonymously. Check your company's code of conduct policy.

- **Respect others** as everyone is different. Some cultures may be taught to be submissive, but that does not mean they cannot be leaders. They may lead in different ways from you, but that does not mean they are not good enough.
- **Get involved in diversity programs** within your firm to act as a force for change. Continue to find ways that these programs can help change the culture of your firm. It may take time but remember, Rome was not built in a day. You may look back five years from now and see the difference.

Speaking up and getting involved in your organization's DE&I programs are so important to affect change. We need to continue to push through to show the impact of the DE&I programs on our organization's culture. We cannot just talk about it; we must do more to ensure people are being treated fairly. Enacting change starts with all of us.

ACTIONS YOU CAN TAKE:

- **Read one book about diversity** – for example:

  o *The Loudest Duck: Moving Beyond Diversity while Embracing Differences to Achieve Success at Work* by Laura A. Liswood
  o *Belonging At Work: Everyday Actions You Can Take to Cultivate an Inclusive Organization* by Rhodes Perry
  o *We Can't Talk about That at Work! How to Talk about Race, Religion, Politics, and Other Polarizing Topics* by Mary-Frances Winters

    o   See more at this site: https://teambuilding.com/blog/diversity-inclusion-books

- **Research your company's business resource group (BRG)** to find a group to get involved with and help make the culture more diverse. Business Resource Groups are voluntary groups within the organizations that serve as a resource for diverse groups. Register for at least one group to make a difference.
- **Become an ally** – If you hear someone being harassed because of their diversity, speak up and let the other person know that it is not appropriate. When you say you are an ally, you need to act the part and become engaged in changing a situation that is adverse.

CHAPTER 15

YES, YOU BELONG IN THAT ROOM!

"Because true belonging only happens when we present our authentic, imperfect selves to the world, our sense of belonging can never be greater than our level of self-acceptance."

Brene Brown, Daring Greatly

Many women do not use their voice often enough in the workplace and it can stall their career. I have learned over the years to push myself to speak up in meetings and use my voice wisely. I am still finding my way to make sure my voice is heard and ensure that what I say matters.

I believe the reason some women do not speak up in meetings is because they think they do not belong in the room. I see this often with women, and sometimes men, in middle management. I know they have a lot to say, but they do not feel comfortable saying it in meetings.

Perception happens quickly. Meaning if you are in a meeting, managers and colleagues will judge you instantly. It can take someone seconds to perceive you in a negative way. If you are sitting in the back or side of the room or maybe taking notes, people may perceive you in the wrong way and it can hurt your career.

Here are some key steps you can take to be more self-assured and feel that you do belong in that room:

1. **Be prepared** – Be sure to always prepare before meetings, especially with senior managers. Talking points and practicing before a presentation can help to minimize your stress and make you feel more at ease.

2. **Be confident** – Do not let your negative self-talk get to you. Remember to be positive about yourself and remind yourself the value that you bring to the organization. Do not forget to smile; this will keep you in a positive mood. Sit up straight so that you look confident.

3. **Be open to learning** – You do not need to be the smartest person in the room. It is okay to admit you do not know everything. Do not let this fear of not-knowing something keep you from going to the room that scares you the most. If you are asked a question that you do not know, you can say "I do not have the answer to this, but I can get back to you."

4. **Define your passion** – Do you know what you are most passionate about at work? If not, take a minute to think about what drives you the most. This will help define your "purpose statement". Think about what makes you feel strongly about the topic you are presenting and how you can do things better for others. Once you do this, it will impact how you show up.

These are just a few steps you can take to turn around that feeling of not belonging. It can be difficult at times, especially in larger corporations, to feel like you do not belong or fit in. Sometimes you may not fit in and that is okay too. If you feel this way, it may be time to look for another job.

In my research on executive presence, I uncovered the role unconscious bias plays. It impacts women the most but can also impact others who may have been raised in different environments or cultures. Many organizations are now focused on DE&I (see Chapter 14), so this should be a part of changing perceptions.

If you think you need help with how others perceive you, seek a mentor or sponsor in your organization. It helps to have someone other than your immediate manager to give you real feedback. They can also give you guidance on your progress. The first step is recognizing how you are showing up. Once you do this, you can take steps towards improvement.

ACTIONS YOU CAN TAKE:

- **Prepare** – For your next meeting, write a short summary of the topic and put down one question you would like to ask. Ensure you have any back up material you need on the topic.
- **Sit at the table**, not the side of the room.
- **Be present** – Do not multitask as this will blindside you when someone asks you a question and you have not been paying attention.

CHAPTER 16

BE AUTHENTIC!

"The privilege of a lifetime is to become who you truly are."

Carl Gustav Jung

I am sure you have heard about the imposter syndrome, especially when you are in the workplace. This occurs when you feel like you must be someone other than yourself to be successful. But you must ask yourself, "Why would I want to be someone else, and not myself?"

Being authentic is the best way to be and will only make you feel better about yourself. Do not let anyone try to tell you that you should be someone that you are not. Not even your manager in your performance review! Remember, your manager is giving you their opinion, and you do not have to agree with it.

Here are some ways you can ensure that you can be yourself, but also be professional:

1. **Be aware of how you behave or present yourself** – Be yourself but ensure that it is respectful of others and maintain professionalism. We talked about having executive presence, but you can still be yourself. I see

senior executives that do not possess executive presence. There is still a bias around executive presence for women and diverse individuals that needs further exploration.

2. **Find your own style**– When I first started working, I always wore suits and tried to have the right trendy bags and shoes. I realize now that what you wear is not what makes you successful. Yes, you should dress appropriately, but there are ways of doing this without spending a lot of money.

3. **Make your voice heard** – You may not agree with what management is doing and that is okay. Do not be afraid to voice your opinion. Management is not always right, so they need to hear feedback. If you keep speaking up about the issues that you feel important about, eventually change will occur. It may not occur overnight, but my feeling is even if it changes for my children's future career, I have made a difference.

4. **Embrace your culture** – Every culture is different, and it is okay to embrace your own. You do not have to pretend that you come from a wealthy family to seem more important. Learn to feel comfortable about your upbringing and background. I grew up in a lower-income family and I am so proud of what I have accomplished.

Everyone is unique, and that is what makes us special. Trying to be like others just makes you seem fake, and I am sure it will not make you happy. You can always develop skills that you do not have, but your personality is yours and you should not change it.

It can be challenging in the workplace when you are trying to get ahead and you are not sure why you may be stalled in a position. Do not let this be the reason you change being who you are. This will only lead to stress and anxiety.

Once you embrace who you are, you begin to have confidence in yourself, even with all your imperfections – and do not worry, everyone has them. When you begin to accept yourself, you will be happier in your career, which will lead to more success.

ACTIONS YOU CAN TAKE:

- **Take inventory of how you show up for work** – Blending your authentic self with professionalism, respect of others and engagement can be challenging but is achievable. Always dress appropriately based on your industry. For example, if you work in finance, it is business casual, and flip-flops, T-shirts and sneakers are not appropriate. Check your company's policy on the dress code to ensure it is appropriate.
- **Ask for feedback on how others perceive you at work** – Sometimes you may not realize how you come across to others.
- **Be yourself** – Have the confidence to be who you are. We are all unique and that is what makes us special.

CHAPTER 17

HOW DO YOU DEAL WITH CHANGE IN YOUR ORGANIZATION?

"The secret of change is to focus all of your energy not on fighting the old, but on building the new."

Socrates

I am sure you have heard the saying, "change is constant". It is true, as change occurs every day. It can be hard to deal with change in the workplace, especially if you have been at a firm for a very long time.

In the asset management industry, we have been dealing with transformation since around 2018. The biggest reasons for this were fee compression and assets going into passive investments like ETFs rather than actively managed investments. The industry had to make changes in order to keep up with competitors and drive expenses down.

Digitization of processes became a big buzzword in the industry. This meant creating digital tools for client self-service portals, while also automating processes done within the company.

Organizations also turned to outsourcing to countries where salaries were much lower, such as India and Hungary.

This has caused a lot of angst for those employees working in the headquarters in big cities across the world, such as New York City, London and Hong Kong. Change was happening and those who did not get on board were at risk for losing their jobs.

Personally, I was put into a new position to transform the client service team within the asset management division of my firm. I was excited about it, but I also was fearful of change. I was given a job that I had never asked for and truly wanted to remain the manager of a team that I loved. I needed to figure out how to handle the change or I would lose my job. I did not do a great job of handling it. I was resentful, depressed and fearful. I did not know how to do transformation. This was very challenging for me to handle.

During this time, others on the team faced the same challenges. Some of the individuals in the team had been with the firm for over 20 years, doing the same work in the same way over that time. They did not want to change.

Was change necessary at this time? Absolutely, as we had so many manual processes, which caused considerable risk to the firm. We also were not operating efficiently, which caused us to have excess headcount and unnecessarily high expenses. For the company to become efficient, we needed to change and improve our way of operating the business.

We had a few individuals who were resistant to change and some who could not handle the stress that came with it. We lost many people in the next couple of years. In 2022 alone, we hired 13 new people to our team. This was also partly due to the impact of the COVID pandemic, and the period known as the "Great Resignation".

It was not an easy time, but the people who remained were passionate about the team and spent time working through the change, training new employees and learning how to manage stress. We were lucky that the head of our team was empathetic, strategic and had our backs with senior management. Having a manager like this was so important, but this of course does not always happen.

While the time was extremely challenging, I came out on the other side with so much that I had learned. I stepped up to the challenge and was able to overcome the feelings that I had and do what was needed for the team. While we did lose some very good people, we also gained people with different ideas, attitudes and knowledge, which was useful for us to develop even more efficient processes throughout the organization.

I can now look back and give you some tips on what I could have done differently from the start to accept the change and become a change agent:

- **Communicate** with management to learn about what their vision is for the future and where you can make the greatest impact.
- **Communicate with your team** and bring them along, making them part of the change.
- **Listen** to seek to understand the "why" around the change.
- **Learn** all you can about the change. Is it a new technology? How can you use your experience and knowledge to develop a new automated process to create efficiencies?
- **Be collaborative** with management, internal stakeholders and your team members to effect change.

This is so important because if you are not collaborative, you will be left behind. See more on collaboration and partnership in Chapter 24.

The people who did not make it through the change were resistant and thought the way they had always done things was the right way. I had to learn the hard way that this was not the case. I did not always like the change that was being made. For example, I thought it was easier to send an email than input information into a workflow. What I failed to realize was that, once you put data into a workflow, you have created efficiencies and you can now create metrics around this data. Metrics help organizations analyze where work volumes are and where they need to focus on inefficiencies. For example, if your employees are saying that they are at capacity, but you have no way of knowing what they are working on. By having this data in your systems, you can run reports to see where the volumes are coming from. It also helps to understand where there is need to automate.

If you are facing transformation at your organization, stop and think about why it is happening. It may be scary, but there is most likely a good reason for why they are making changes. Companies need to transform their business to meet the demands of their clients. If they do not change fast enough, they are in jeopardy of going out of business.

There are multiple examples of companies that did not survive because they did not change their business models. *Blockbuster* is one of the best examples of this. Simon Sinek talks about this in his book, *Infinite Game.* "The then CEO of Blockbuster recommended to the board that they needed to change their business model, but the board did not allow that because they were making most of their money from late fees. They had a finite mindset." A finite mindset is when you view situations as either win or lose. An infinite mindset is grateful, builds relationships and works toward the common good. When you lead with an infinite mindset, you can change the rules, evolve strategies, and learn and grow as a team.

As times were changing from video to digital, *Blockbuster* failed to change with them. Netflix at the time was up and coming, and even invited *Blockbuster* to invest in their company. *Blockbuster* refused and the rest is history. They only have one store left in the country today.

ACTIONS YOU CAN TAKE:

- **Find out what your company's purpose is** – Most companies have a mission statement with a vision. Purpose statements are becoming a new thing after Simon Sinek's book *Start with Why*.
- **Become solution-oriented** – If you see processes within your organization that could be done more efficiently or automated, speak to your manager to see how you can change the process. If you are solution-oriented in this changing world, you will make a valuable impact to your organization.
- **Be a change agent** – Follow the steps that I outlined above on how you can be a change agent. Having individuals that are change agents can assist management in helping to turn their team's mindset around.

CHAPTER 18

FAIL FORWARD

"Success is not final; failure is not fatal; it is the courage to continue that counts."

Winston Churchill

I am often a perfectionist, especially at work. I want things to go according to plan and be successful. When that does not happen, it makes me anxious and upset with myself. I do not like this feeling.

No one ever likes to fail because it may make them seem as if they are not successful or smart. This is so far from the truth. I once was part of a project that had a failed process, and it was a real eye opener for me. For the most part, the project was successful, but it did have one process that did not go as planned. Some called it a failure. I became upset with myself because I did not want to be associated with failure. But then I looked at the situation, and I realized that we did not fail, because we learned a valuable lesson. We learned that there were multiple steps that we needed to look at before implementation. We didn't start with a project plan that would have allowed us to look at all the downstream processes that may be affected by the change.

I have heard of so many successful people who have failed when they first started out. Do you know that Thomas Edison was told by his teachers that he was too stupid to learn anything? Albert Einstein did not start speaking until he was four. Oprah Winfrey was fired from her first job as a TV anchor. Stephen King's novel *Carrie* was rejected 30 times. I could go on and on about people who are now successful and the number of times that they failed before. We have all failed at some point in our lives. But failure is not fatal!

Here are some tips on how you can "fail forward" to success:

1. **Admit mistakes** – Have you ever failed at something and then not be able to admit that you were wrong? This is a mistake. If you know that you have failed or were wrong, you should admit it and then learn the lesson. There is no point in deflecting blame as it will only make you look bad. Accepting your mistakes will allow you to move forward to fix them.

2. **Learn the lesson and apply it the next time** – I love doing a post-mortem on an initiative that did not go as planned. What went wrong? What could I have done better to make this a success? These kinds of lessons will only help you for your next project.

3. **Get back up** – Do not let failure keep you down. You need to get right back to doing what you do. Failure is not a life sentence. You can look at failure as an opportunity to do something else or something better.

4. **Take risks again** – Whenever you take risks, it can lead to failure. That is what risk-taking means. However, even if you fail, continue to take risks, because there is always the chance that they can turn into success. If you believe in what you are doing and you are planning with

controls in place to mitigate the risks, your plan can be successful.

The scientists and medical experts who worked on creating a new vaccine for COVID can be seen as an example of how failing forward works in practice. They needed to do many tests before the vaccine was successful. Each time they produced a new vaccine, they were able to learn what they needed to do differently for the next batch to be even more successful.

This concept of failing forward should be taught more often in schools and organizations. While we always want to be successful, failure is often the first step to getting there.

The next time you fail look at it as a learning opportunity that can help push you forward to success.

ACTIONS YOU CAN TAKE:

- **Analyze** your recent projects or one you are currently working on. What could you have done differently or better that would have made it a success?
- **What was the lesson learned?** Make sure you enhance your process in the future. All missteps can turn your next project into a success.
- **Take a risk** – Is there something that you really wanted to try, but you are afraid to fail at? How about trying it out? I am taking a risk with my coaching business and writing this book. They might turn into failures. But what if they do not?

CHAPTER 19

DON'T LET REJECTION STOP YOU FROM DOING WHAT YOU LOVE

"Every time I thought I was being rejected from something good, I was actually being re-directed to something better."

Steve Maraboli

Have you ever gone for a position that you knew you would be perfect for, but you did not get? We have all been there at some point in our lives. It hurts especially when we feel we deserve the position.

Unfortunately, life is not always fair. You can feel bad, but do not stay there for too long. Here are some things I have done to change my mindset after being rejected from a position:

- **Analyze why you did not get the position** – Maybe you were not the best person for the job and that is okay. Or maybe you were the right person, but the hiring manager wanted someone else. You should ask the hiring manager for feedback so you can understand why the decision was made.

- **Learn** – After you get feedback (which you may or may not agree with), think about how you may be able to develop your skills. There are now many online certification programs you can take. For me, taking the leadership course from Wharton was life changing. It was so insightful, and I learned things I never thought about before. I wish I had taken this many years ago. I highly recommend you investigate one of these courses today. Some companies also offer tuition reimbursement.
- **Prioritize yourself** – Learning new skills is one way to do this, but when I say, "prioritize yourself", I mean putting yourself first when it comes to your career. Think about what you really want to do. It is not about what others want you to do. Write down what your vision is for your future. You may find that you did not even want that job you went for after all.

We are all unique, with different strengths and development areas. Do not think, because you did not get the job or the promotion, that you are not good enough. You are good enough and you will get the job you are passionate about in your own time.

When you focus on your goals and vision, it helps you understand where you can be impactful, and this may actually be where you are now. Think about how you can do what you are passionate about even in your current position.

Do not wait until you find the perfect job in order to do what makes you happy. Do it now, and in time you will find the role that you deserve.

ACTIONS YOU CAN TAKE:

- **Pause and think** about why you may have been rejected. Most likely, it is not about you.
- **Ask for feedback** – I know I say this a lot but asking for feedback is the best way to understand why you were rejected.
- **Move forward** – It is okay to be down about the rejection or grieve for what you no longer have, but do not stay in that place. Look at steps that can help you move forward.

CHAPTER 20

"WAIT UNTIL I'M FINISHED SPEAKING, PLEASE!"

"First, let me finish. Then interrupt."

Brian Spellman

I read an article by best-selling author and psychologist Adam Grant on how most men interrupt women when they are speaking. Adam wrote "When people make claims about behavior in groups, my job as an organizational psychologist is to look at the evidence. The pattern is clear and consistent: It's usually men who won't shut up. Especially powerful men."

This article details a study done on US Senators, who had demonstrated leadership roles, seniority and influence, spent more time on the senate floor, but only if they were a man. It also references an experiment that shows women are more afraid of being perceived as controlling when they do speak up.

The article really resonated with me because I have noticed this pattern of behavior in the workplace. It seems to be even more noticeable now, with Zoom meetings.

Women are either told they are too aggressive when they speak up or that they are not strategic when they keep quiet. It can be a real challenge for women in the workplace. I am not calling out all men, but I would ask them to think about this behavior when they are in meetings.

While we cannot control how people behave, we can control how we react to the behavior. Here are some suggestions for dealing with this type of behavior:

- **Ask for respect** – When you are making a presentation, ask upfront for everyone to save their questions to the end. When people interrupt the speaker, the meeting can go off the rails very quickly. Asking for respect upfront allows for a smoother presentation and gives everyone a chance to hear what you have to say.
- **Ask to be heard** – Ask interrupters to please wait until you finish speaking. Sometimes they will not listen but try to be insistent in telling them to wait until you are finished. At some point, they should get the hint.
- **Give feedback** – I find giving feedback right away to the interrupter works. It may be politely asking them in the meeting to wait until the end to ask questions or you can call them afterwards to give them the feedback. They do not always realize what they are doing. Reminding them that it is not respectful to you should stop the behavior from happening again.
- **Report poor behavior** – If you find the same person continues to interrupt you in meetings even after you have given feedback, it is time to report it to your manager or theirs. The behavior may not change, but at least you have voiced your concern.

Organizations should not tolerate this behavior and should hold people accountable. They do not always do this, and many organizations expect people to just get along. However, this will not happen if the behavior is allowed to continue.

Women need to speak up more when they see this kind of behavior. Yes, it can be scary, with the risk of retaliation. If you are afraid to speak to the person directly, speak to your manager or the person's manager. Every time we speak up about these issues, we are not only making things better for ourselves, but also making things better for the women of the future.

ACTIONS YOU CAN TAKE:

- **Ask your audience to keep questions to the end** – For the next meeting where you are presenting, remember to ask people to keep their questions until the end. This should reduce interruptions.
- **Hold people accountable** – If the same people continue to interrupt you, take them aside and speak to them about how it makes you feel. Let them know that you will not tolerate it any longer and you will escalate if the behavior does not stop.

CHAPTER 21

TAKE YOUR EGO OUT OF IT!

"All you need to know and observe in yourself is this: Whenever you feel superior or inferior to anyone, that's the ego in you."

Eckhart Tolle

Have you ever tried to make others look bad, so you look good? This happens a lot in the corporate world. There is no reason for it. If you are smart, knowledgeable and work hard, you will get ahead, but you should not try to get ahead at the expense of others.

Our ego can really harm our relationships at work as it can undermine how we collaborate with others. The way we think about ourselves and the way we work with others can really help or hinder how effective we are in our jobs.

Here are a few things to think about when your ego seems to get in the way:

- **Did someone just get that job you wanted?** If you take your ego out of it and be happy for the other person, it will not hurt as much. Yes, you really wanted that job, but maybe the other person was just more qualified. There will be other jobs for you to focus on.

- **Are you partnering with someone at work on a big initiative?** Does the other person send emails to senior managers, making them think they are doing all the work? This can and does happen, but so what if it does? Do not quit because you feel you are not being recognized. Take a step back and take your ego out of it. If you value the work you are doing and you know that you are doing a great job, let the other person do their thing. It does not have to stop you from doing your thing. Raise your voice and remind people of the work you are doing and the partnerships that you have with others.

- **Are you working with someone who is junior to you?** This is a great time to focus on letting this person shine. How can you help this person become successful? Let them take the lead. It will not hurt you to take a step back to give someone else a chance.

We all have egos, but some are bigger than others. It is important to recognize when your ego may be getting in the way of your relationships. Think about the ways you can work with others. Are you giving the other person a chance, or are you treating them as your personal assistant? When I work with others, I try to partner with them because this is the best way to get a job done, and get it done well. Fighting and squabbling with others are only going to cause delays in your projects.

Working with others can be difficult because people can be competitive. Being competitive is fine, as long as you play fair. I learned from Simon Sinek, author of *The Infinite Games*, that it is better to have a "worthy rival" than constantly working to win and being better than others. Being worthy rivals leads to innovation, which only helps to take your company to the next level.

Can you try taking your ego out of the game and see how you feel? I bet you will feel a whole lot better. Just think about the ways we could work better if we partnered together, rather than working against each other.

ACTIONS YOU CAN TAKE:

- **Say thank you** – Think about some of the projects you are currently working on. Are you collaborating with others? Try to give acknowledgements this week to the others in your working group. Thank them for their partnership.
- **Find a Worthy Rival** – Do you have a worthy rival? You may think of them now as a "frenemy". Try asking them to have coffee this week to discuss ways you can partner together rather than working against each other.
- **Become a mentor** – Is there a junior person on your team who could use your guidance? Take it upon yourself to ask them if they need any additional training or mentoring. One small step can really help a junior person who may be struggling to find their way.

CHAPTER 22

HANDLING HYBRID AND REMOTE WORK IN OUR NEW NORMAL

"Success in a hybrid work environment requires employers to move beyond viewing remote or hybrid environments as a temporary or short-term strategy and treat it as an opportunity."

George Penn, Managing Vice President, Gartner

After having worked from home for over two years during the COVID pandemic, many people found it hard to come back to the office. Return to the office, or RTTO, became the new buzzword. CEOs from the largest companies had a lot to say about wanting employees back in the office. It is almost humorous that this has become such a big issue for some. If anything, large companies could look at reducing real estate and set up certain functions to be remote or hybrid. This would certainly decrease spending and create efficiencies.

But unfortunately, many CEOs, especially in the finance industry, have decided that they want employees back in the office. They think that employees are more productive in the office and can be more creative in person. While I do agree that there is a certain element of working in person that can help generate innovative ideas, I have also seen this done well remotely during COVID.

We now have a new generation of employees who started their careers working from home, and many appear to like it a lot. However, many firms insist on a hybrid working pattern and require employees to spend more time in the office, and if you are not meeting the quota, it could mean a reduction in pay or an impact on your promotion opportunities.

If you are finding yourself in this situation, there are a few things you can do to ensure that you are still happy in your career:

- **Compromise** – Considering that, before COVID, most employees worked in the office full-time, hybrid is not a bad alternative. In a hybrid situation, you may be allowed to work from home two days a week. At the time of this writing, there are a few firms that are requiring four days in the office. Every company has their own specific rules, so it is important to understand their rules.
- **Decide** – If you prefer to work from home, you need to decide if you are at the right company. Maybe another industry would work better for you. A lot of tech companies and consumer products still allow remote working.
- **Negotiate** – If you are a high performer, you may be able to negotiate a deal with your company. I have seen a few employees being based in other states and it seems to work well for them. You need to keep your performance up though if you want this to succeed. The other issue is if new management comes in, they may tell you the jig is up.

These are some decisions employees must make on their own as it does not look like organizations are going to change their policy, whether it is right or wrong. This of course may change down the road, especially when those who started their career during COVID begin to move into leadership roles. They may find cost-efficient ways to make remote working more attainable.

ACTIONS YOU CAN TAKE:

- **Be open to compromise** if you are not ready to look for another job
- **Decide** what type of environment you want to be
- **Negotiate** – Ask if there are any ways you can change the model so that it works for you.

CHAPTER 23

NETWORKING INSIDE AND OUTSIDE YOUR ORGANIZATION

"Courage starts with showing up and letting ourselves be seen."

Brene Brown

I can't tell you enough how important networking is in order to meet the right people who can support you in your career. I will also admit that I do not do this well enough even to this day after working over 30 years, but I am including this because I do think it is so important for you to do.

After doing some research and watching others who have been successful with networking, I have put together a few tips for you.

- **Join internal groups** - I mentioned BRG Groups in Chapter 14. These are excellent ways to meet people in your organization both up and down the organization. Typically, they will have an event with various individuals giving a presentation on a relevant topic. After the events, most will also have a cocktail reception. This is the time that you can meet other individuals.

It is not always easy to go up to people you do not know. If you are an introvert like me, it is even harder. I have practiced different ways to go up to individuals I want to meet especially senior managers. It helps to have a topic or a plan before you go up to them. In a recent networking event, I went up to the CEO of our line of business to say hello and I also introduced a colleague of mine to him. We ended up having a 10-minute conversation.

This is just one way to do it. There are other ways to speak to others you may be afraid to speak to. You can comment about someone's outfit or asking them how they are doing is a very easy first step. I always find if you ask others questions about themselves it makes it easier because everyone likes to talk about themselves.

A few easy questions you can ask include –

Where did you go to college?
How long have you been at the firm?
Can you talk about your journey in becoming successful at the firm?

- **Set up meetings or coffee chats** – I find if you want to meet someone, you can easily set up a meeting or invite them for coffee. And yes, you can do this virtually as well through Microsoft Teams or Zoom. These can be informal meetings or formal if you are meeting with a senior manager. If you are setting up a meeting with a senior manager, make sure you have an agenda or a plan for what you want to speak with them about.
- **External networking** – It is also important to meet external people because you never know when you may be looking for another job. There are various industry events or conferences that you can attend. You may be

able to find these in LinkedIn or you may receive emails directly from the coordinators of these events.

I have gone to a few of these events during my career and have formed some great relationships. I have also been a participant at an asset management conference where I hosted an entire session. It was such a great learning experience.

If you are looking to grow your career, networking is a big part of it. It definitely helps to know the right people especially when there may be an opportunity in their team. Remember, it is not just knowing the right people, but making sure their perception of you is a good one. Make sure you are prepared for meeting them, ask the right questions and let them know where your interests lay.

ACTION STEPS YOU CAN TAKE:

- **Join an internal or external event to attend** – before the event, pick out 1 or 2 people that you would like to speak to. Prepare an intro sentence and a few questions to ask them.
- **Set up an internal coffee chat** – select 1 or 2 people that you would like to meet to get to know them and for them to get to know you better.
- **Prepare your elevator pitch** – it is important to have an elevator pitch so the next time you are in the elevator with a senior manager, you can be prepared to say hello and chat with them. I was recently in the elevator with a very senior manager and I looked at her and said hello. That was it! I missed the chance to get to know her better and for her to get to know me. Don't make the same mistake I did.

CHAPTER 24

COLLABORATION AND PARTNERSHIP

"Alone we can do so little; together we can do so much."
Helen Keller

One important area in the workplace that took me a little time to learn was collaborating and partnering with colleagues. This is so important especially when working on projects that are across teams. If you do not partner with others, it could impact your project negatively and cause you unnecessary stress.

I remember working on a project several years ago where all the participants in the working group did not get along. One of the reasons they didn't get along is because they each wanted to be the lead on the project. They would do things to sabotage the others in the working group. For example, one participant would email the senior manager separately. By doing this, the senior manager would see them as the lead on the project. When others in the working group found out, they weren't happy. After that, no one in the working group trusted each other and the project failed.

In order to help your project succeed, here a few steps you can take –

- **Define roles & responsibilities** – set up a plan for what each participant is responsible for doing. This will help when you create the implementation plan so that you will have an owner for each step in the process. It also will hold each participant accountable for their part of the project.
- **Create an implementation plan** – this is so important in managing any project. Outline each key step in the project that will help meet your target date. Manage the plan weekly to ensure you are making progress.
- **Set up recurring meetings with working group** – this will ensure that each participant in the project has a voice and is adding value to the project. Allow each participant to give their update and give feedback on the direction of the project.
- **Status Updates** – Agree with the working group on status updates to senior management. It could be a weekly or monthly status update with the key deliverables.

These steps will help to keep the project on track and the group working together as a team. Of course, you cannot always keep a rogue participant from trying to look like the one who is doing all the work.

I find by building relationships with everyone in the working group helps form the partnership and allows you to work collaboratively. View everyone on the team as a key to making the project successful. In Chapter 21, I talked about keeping your ego out of it. Remember the project isn't about you, it is an initiative to help your team, the firm or your clients.

ACTION STEPS YOU CAN TAKE:

- **Set up the project for success** - If you are currently working on a project, take time to ensure you have the right implementation plan and defined roles and responsibilities.
- **Build relationships** - Get to know the others in the working group. Set up calls or intro meetings. Even if you are not working on a project, it is helpful to get to know others in your stakeholder teams – see Chapter 23 on networking.

CHAPTER 25

TAKE YOUR VACATION!

"Almost everything will work if you unplug it for a few minutes ... including you."

Anne Lamott

The Jersey Shore is one of my favorite vacation spots. Every year in July or August, I go there to recharge and think about my goals for the rest of the year. One of my recent vacations was one of the best at the Jersey Shore as it was one of first times in many years that I did not look at my work email for most of the time. I only checked email in the morning or in the evening, not during the day when I was enjoying the time with my family.

Why did I feel the need to check my email in the past? I guess it was the fear of missing out – yes, FOMO! I have learned that I suffer from that.

I believe FOMO comes from being busy every moment of every day during my work week. I am sure many of you are the same. It is one of the reasons that most people are addicted to their phones. Also, we do not like to be bored. I remember thinking how great the phone was when I realized that I no longer was going to be bored when I had to wait in a line at the store or wherever I was. How crazy is that?

During my vacation, instead of reading my emails, I found other things to keep me busy. I love to read fiction books while I am sitting on the beach. Fiction books are great because they take you to another place or another world. They allow you to escape whatever you are facing in your current environment. I am sure there are many of you out there who need an escape.

I also love to read nonfiction books, especially self-help books. It was something that began when I was in my twenties. Whenever I had a problem, I turned to books. It really helps to get another person's perspective on how you can change your life or a situation you find yourself in.

I read a couple of nonfiction books during my vacation that I want to share because they have really helped me with my mindset and how I will approach life going forward. Yes, they were that good! The first book I read was *Positive Intelligence* written by Shirzad Chamine, which I mentioned previously. I not only read his book, but I enrolled in his seven-week training program. It was introduced to me by one of my coaching colleagues. I told her that she had been instrumental in changing my life just by sharing this program with me. See Chapter 8.

The second book I read was *Instant Calm* by Karen Salmansohn. It is a short book that you can read in an hour but refer to over and over. It gives you instructions on how to do two-minute meditations.

As I was reading this book, it occurred to me that the meditations that Karen was instructing me to do were very similar to the PQ reps Shiraz talks about. PQ reps are two minutes, five minutes or twelve minutes, and they focus on breathing, vision and touch.

Instant Calm shares quick vision and touch meditations as well as smell, sound and movement. Karen also offers training and personal coaching (see https://www.notsalmon.com/notsalmon-story/).

These are all great ways to change your mindset, which in turn can change your life. Whenever I learn new things that I find life changing, I must share them.

Remember, take your vacation now. It just may be life-changing!

CHAPTER 26

DON'T LET OTHERS IN THE WORKPLACE STEAL YOUR POWER

"The most common way people give up their power is by thinking they don't have any."

Alice Walker

"Don't let anyone steal your power!" One of my managers said this to me before she retired, and for some reason it stuck with me. It is so true. Every one of us has their own power, and no one can take it away from us unless we let them.

After I took the "Executive Presence" course, I thought a lot about myself and my confidence level. While I know that I am smart, creative, logical and bring value to my organization, I still struggle with confidence. I do not know why I still feel this way. As I mentioned a few times throughout this book, I have experienced many setbacks: I was moved to a position I did not want, I was overlooked for a promotion on my team, and I had critical functions moved away from me. It hurt a lot and I felt like I was invisible. It also impacted my confidence.

In one meeting, a senior manager who was sitting right next to me and knew all the work I had been doing on an initiative, singled out my boss as the one who would help the team drive the project. He did not mention me at all, even though he knew that I had already done a lot of great work on the initiative. It was hurtful and he probably did not even realize it. This happens often in the workplace.

You may find yourself in situations like this. I recommend to not sit back and let it slide. We must speak up for ourselves to maintain our power. Even if you need to remind others of all the work you did. Use your power to do this! I have realized that I cannot stay in a place that does not recognize my values. It is not good for my mental health. I continue to look for opportunities where I can a be in a place where I'm passionate about the work I do, recognized for the value I bring and love the people with whom I work alongside. For me, if I have all these things, then I am successful!

I wrote this book to share the challenges that I have gone through in the hope that this will help guide you through your challenges and allow you to face them head-on without being blindsided. It can be hard to find people whom you can trust in the workplace, and this book will help guide you to where you want to be. My hope for you is to find the success your desire.

Here's to your success!

Rene

RESOURCES

1. "**The Infinite Game**", Simon Sinek
2. "**Start with Why**", Simon Sinek
3. "**Positive Intelligence**", Shirzad Charmine
4. "**The history and growth of the diversity equity and inclusion profession**" , Sarah Dong; 2021
5. "**Handling Diversity in the Workplace**", Based on the book Handling Diversity in the Workplace Communication is the Key by Kay duPont,CSP; Copyright 1999 American Media Inc. All Rights Reserved https://www.ars.usda.gov/ARSUserFiles/30420000/NewEmployeeResources/Handling%20Diversity%20in%20the%20Workplace.pdf
6. **Instant Calm**, Karen Salmansohn
7. **Wharton Executive Leadership Program,** Executive Presence and Persuasive Leadership Program
8. **Toxic Workplace Cultures Hurt Workers and Company Profits**, Beth Mirza (see https://www.shrm.org/resourcesandtools/hr-topics/employee-relations/pages/toxic-workplace-culture-report.aspx).
9. **Who won't shut up in meetings? Men say it's women. It's not**, Adam Grant (see https://www.washingtonpost.com/outlook/2021/02/18/men-interrupt-women-tokyo-olympics/)
10. **Happy Equal Pay Day? Here are 6 charts showing why it's not much of a celebration.**, Chabelli Carrazan, https://19thnews.org/author/chabeli-carrazana

Can You Help?

Thank You for Reading My Book!

I really appreciate all your feedback, and I love hearing what you have to say.

I need your input to make the next version of this book and my future books better.

Please leave me an honest review on Amazon letting me know what you thought of the book.

Thanks so much!

Rene Madden

AUTHOR'S BIO

Introducing Rene, a multi-faceted professional with a passion for personal growth and professional excellence. With a diverse background spanning over three decades in the asset management industry, Rene brings a wealth of experience and expertise to her role as an Executive Director at a prestigious Asset Management firm.

Rene's journey is a testament to her unwavering commitment to continuous improvement and development. Holding a BS degree in Accounting from Saint Joseph's University in Philadelphia, PA, Rene's academic foundation laid the groundwork for her illustrious career. Her commitment to the teams she has managed over the years has been instrumental in her success, allowing her to expertly navigate the intricacies of the asset management landscape while also helping her team to be successful.

Beyond her impressive career achievements, Rene is a certified Professional Coach, having honed her coaching skills through rigorous training from Coach Training Alliance (CTA). This additional dimension to her skill set enables her to empower individuals and teams to reach their full potential, fostering growth and resilience.

Rene's dedication to personal growth led her to the Positive Intelligence (PQ) Coach Workshop, where she had the privilege of learning from renowned author and coach, Shirzad Charmine, in July 2020. This experience further solidified her belief in the power of positive mindset and emotional intelligence as catalysts for transformation.

In May 2023, Rene added another feather to her cap by completing the Executive Presence and Influence: Persuasive Leadership Development Program at Wharton, an accomplishment that reflects her commitment to mastering the art of influential leadership.

With a distinctive blend of financial expertise, coaching proficiency, and a penchant for continuous learning, Rene is a true trailblazer. Her unique journey and multifaceted skill set make her a sought-after thought leader, an inspiration to her colleagues and clients, and a catalyst for positive change in both her professional and personal spheres.

ACKNOWLEDGEMENTS

There are so many people that I would like to thank who have helped me and guided me through this process of writing this book and then getting it published.

First, my husband, Gene Madden, who had to listen to me for the last 30 years while I faced many challenges in the workplace. He was my sounding board through it all. It wasn't easy for him, but he was always there for me through thick and thin.

Second, my previous manager, Stacey Panagakis, who was a real inspiration to me. She taught me so much in the 5 years that I worked for her, and she really helped me to see where my opportunities were to grow and develop in my career. She gave me direct and honest feedback that I had never received before. She also took time to read my book and gave me helpful, constructive feedback.

Finally, I would like to thank my children who give me the strength and courage to go through life every day and be a boss! My co-workers who I love to work with every day, and I want to continue to partner with them so they can achieve the success they desire. My beta readers (Kishor Kshatriya, Beth Barry, Jodi Sally and Danielle Azua) who were kind enough to read my book before it went to publishing. And special thanks to Donella Looger who I met through a Writer's FaceBook group. She was godsend as she gave me very valuable feedback!

www.ingramcontent.com/pod-product-compliance
Lightning Source LLC
Chambersburg PA
CBHW070726130626
46553CB00005B/2167